Contents

Reading for TODAY

Workbook Three

PROGRAM AUTHORS

Linda Ward Beech • **Tara McCarthy**

PROGRAM CONSULTANTS

Myra K. Baum
Office of Adult and
    Continuing Education
Brooklyn, New York

Francis J. Feltman, Jr.
Racine Youth Offender
    Correctional Facility
Racine, Wisconsin

Mary Ann Guilliams
Gary Job Corps
San Marcos, Texas

Julie Jacobs
Inmate Literacy Project
Santa Clara County Library
Milpitas, California

Maxine L. McCormick
Workforce Education
Orange County Public Schools
Orlando, Florida

Sandra S. Owens
Laurens County Literacy Council
Laurens, South Carolina

STECK-VAUGHN
ELEMENTARY·SECONDARY·ADULT·LIBRARY

A Harcourt Company

www.steck-vaughn.com

Acknowledgments

STAFF CREDITS

Executive Editor: Ellen Northcutt

Senior Editor: Donna Townsend

Supervising Designer: Pamela Heaney

Designer: Jessica Bristow

ILLUSTRATION CREDITS: Scott Bieser, Holly Cooper

To the Instructor

The *Reading for Today* workbooks are designed to accompany the new structure of the *Reading for Today* student books. Books 1–6 have corresponding workbooks that follow the same format in:

- controlled vocabulary
- reading level
- phonics and word-building skills
- sight vocabulary
- writing and comprehension skills

Student Book ➡	Workbook
UNIT CONTENTS	**UNIT CONTENTS**
• Discussion	• Discussion
• Sight words	• Reading practice
• Phonics skills	• Phonics generalizations
• Writing skills	• Writing applications
• Reading selection	• Extended reading selection
• Comprehension questions	• Comprehension questions
• Life-coping skills	• Writing practice

The chart shows how a typical unit in a *Reading for Today* workbook serves as a follow-up for its corresponding unit in a *Reading for Today* student book.

Students who use the *Reading for Today* workbooks, however, do not simply review, practice, and reinforce sight words, phonics, and writing skills. Students also extend their learning. They read additional adult-related stories that are written with the controlled vocabulary that puts the reading within their grasp. Students discuss what they bring of their own experience to the reading selections by responding to purpose-setting questions, thus sharpening their thinking and discussion skills. And students write, both to demonstrate comprehension and to respond in their own way to the reading selections.

Teaching Suggestions

Each unit in the *Reading for Today* workbooks follows the pattern outlined below.

Reading and Discussing   Page 3

Objectives: To help the student see the connection between reading and speaking. To improve comprehension through discussion.

Teaching Steps:

A. Read the question or questions. Encourage the learner to talk about the question. Discussing the question will help the student get ready to read the story that follows.

B. Help the student read the story. Remember to praise the learner's efforts.

C. Talk about the story. Help the student answer the discussion question that follows the story. Reread the story if necessary.

Review Words Page 4

Objective: To review the sight words introduced in previous units.

Teaching Steps: Be sure the student understands the directions for each exercise. Have students check their answers by referring to the Answer Key at the back of the book.

Sight Words Page 5

Objectives: To review the sight words learned in the corresponding student book unit. To practice reading word groups or phrases rather than individual words.

Teaching Steps:

A. Help the student read and reread each phrase until each one is smooth and natural. Move your hand or a pencil in an arc under each phrase as the learner reads, to help "push" the reader toward fluency. Praise the learner's success.

B. Help the student fill in the blanks correctly.

C. Practice reading the entire story for fluency. Rereading the story after practicing the phrasing will give the learner a sense of success.

Phonics Practice Pages 6 and 7

Objective: To review and reinforce the phonics skills taught in the student book.

Teaching Steps: Be sure the learner understands the directions for each exercise. Have students check their answers by referring to the Answer Key at the back of the book.

Writing Skills Page 8

Objective: To review and reinforce the writing skills taught in the student book.

Teaching Steps: Help the learner understand the directions for each exercise. Have students check their answers by referring to the Answer Key at the back of the book.

Comprehension Page 9

Objectives: To read the conclusion of the story and answer comprehension questions in writing.

Teaching Steps:

A. Have the student read the story.

B. Have the student write the answers to the questions. The following hints will help the learner succeed.
   1. The answer to the question may often be found stated directly in the story.
   2. Rereading the story after reading a question may make it easier to answer the question.
   3. Some questions can be answered by turning the question into a statement and completing the statement with the answer from the story.

From Reading to Writing Page 10

Objectives: To give students an opportunity to write about their own lives or life experiences. To reinforce reading by writing something for someone else to read.

Teaching Steps:

A. Encourage the learner to get as many ideas or thoughts on paper as possible. Praise any legitimate attempts to write. Try for more clarity only as your student gains confidence in writing.

B. When your student finishes writing, you may wish to go back over the writing and follow the suggestions in Part B of each writing page.

Unit One
Communicating with Others

READING AND DISCUSSING

A. Talk about it.

Do you get tapes from friends or family?

B. Read the story.

Talk on Tape

The sun was down. Ted was home from work. He was playing a tape, and he was laughing. Was it music that made him laugh? Not this time. It was his sister Nell.

Nell had sent Ted a tape. She was telling Ted about the family. Ted's brother hit three home runs. Mom had a job she liked a lot. Dad was feeling well and was going back to work.

Ted has a job and a home in the city. His family is in the country. Nell sends a lot of tapes to Ted. Getting a tape helps Ted when he feels homesick.

C. Think about it.

Have you made a tape for someone?
What did you talk about?

3

A. Read the words from the list. Write the words into the puzzle.

goods
old
some
music
time
quit

¹o
l
²g   ³d   ⁴q
⁵m
⁶

B. Draw a line to match each word and its opposite.

1. lose

2. won't

3. help

a. will

b. hurt

c. find

C. Use the number code to write the words.

a	b	c	d	e	f	g	h	i	j	k	l	m
1	2	3	4	5	6	7	8	9	10	11	12	13

n	o	p	q	r	s	t	u	v	w	x	y	z
14	15	16	17	18	19	20	21	22	23	24	25	26

7   21   9   20   1   18

_____guitar_____

16   12   1   14

_____

20   18   15   21   2   12   5

_____

13   21   19   9   3

_____

17   21   9   20

_____

12   15   19   5

_____

A. Read the phrases in the box aloud. Practice until you can read them smoothly.

1. see the value of Nell's tapes
2. take his time
3. records on tape what is going on
4. has a cold
5. in a shop that sells videos

B. Write the phrases to complete the story.

Ted can _____see the value of Nell's tapes_____.
1

When he gets a tape from Nell, Ted likes to _____
2

_____ playing it. Nell _____
3

_____ in the family.

Nell tells Ted that Dad _____
4

_____. Mom has a job _____
5

_____. Ted's brother Jake

has a guitar and is making some money playing in a band.

When Ted gets a tape from Nell, he feels like he is back

home with the family.

C. Read the story aloud. Practice until you can read it smoothly.

A. Read the words in the list. They all have the short e sound. Write other words with the short e sound. Read them.

bell
Dell
Nell
yell
fed
bed
sent
met
lend
record

1. b + end = ___bend___

2. l + et = _____

3. t + ent = _____

4. r + ed = _____

5. sh + ell = _____

B. Read the word pairs aloud. Circle the words with the short e sound. Write them.

1. (fell)   feel   ___fell___

2. see   sell   _____

3. bet   be   _____

4. feed   fed   _____

5. web   we   _____

C. Read the sentences. Circle the words with the short e sound. Write them.

1. (Ted) likes to (get) tapes from home.   ___Ted___   ___get___

2. He feels good at the end of a tape.   _____

3. The tapes tell Ted his family is OK.   _____

   _____

4. His mother and brother are well.   _____

5. The tapes help Ted when he feels homesick.

   _____   _____   _____

rake
bake
shake
lake
age
pay
radio
table
mistake
they

A. Read the words in the list. They all have the long <u>a</u> sound. Write other words with the long <u>a</u> sound. Read them.

1. c + ake = _____

2. p + age = _____

3. f + ake = _____

4. sh + ape = _____

5. st + age = _____

B. Read the word pairs aloud. Circle the words with the long <u>a</u> sound. Write them.

1. sake   sad   _____

2. talk   tables   _____

3. wage   wag   _____

4. cap   cape   _____

5. plan   play   _____

C. Read the sentences. Circle the words with the long <u>a</u> sound. Write them.

1. Nell makes notes about the family. _____

2. She uses her notes for Ted's tapes. _____

3. It takes time to do them well. _____

4. The tapes go to Ted in the city. _____

5. Ted plays the tapes for his friend Pat.

_____   _____

A. Write and read the new words.

1. sun + set = _____sunset_____

2. cat + walk = _____

3. sand + lot = _____

4. home + sick = _____

5. bed + time = _____

6. out + let = _____

7. work + out = _____

B. Find the two words that make up each word. Write the two words.

1. sometimes _____some_____ _____times_____

2. sundown _____ _____

3. upset _____ _____

4. inside _____ _____

5. videotape _____ _____

6. somewhere _____ _____

7. tonight _____ _____

C. Read the paragraph. Circle the compound words.

Where was the (videotape) from Nell? Did Ted lose it?
He was upset. He had planned to look at it tonight.

When Ted is upset, going for a run sometimes helps.
So Ted got his workout bag. The tape was inside the bag!

Comprehension

A. Read the rest of the story.

Talk on Tape

Ted likes talking to Mrs. Lake. She is an older woman, and her eyes are going bad. Ted wants to help if he can.

"I can't read like I did," she told Ted. "Glasses help me some, but not a lot."

Ted feels that he can help Mrs. Lake. Tapes from Nell helped Ted when he was homesick. Maybe tapes can help Mrs. Lake.

Ted goes to a bookstore and finds books on tape. He buys books about cooking and books about home safety. He buys books that will make Mrs. Lake laugh.

Mrs. Lake uses the tapes all the time. They make her eyes light up. The tapes Ted gives Mrs. Lake have a value that is not about money at all.

B. Write the answers to the questions. Use complete sentences.

1. What is Mrs. Lake's problem?

Mrs. Lake likes to read, but she doesn't see well.

_____

2. Who helps Mrs. Lake?

_____

_____

3. How does this person help Mrs. Lake?

_____

_____

_____

A. Write your own story. You can use your own idea or find one in the box. You may want to use the phrases below in your story.

Subjects

Tapes	Family	Friends
tapes of music	brothers and sisters	helping someone
talk tapes	to be homesick	plans to see friends
a tape store	going home	feeling down or up
good videotapes	take time out	eating out
value for money	holidays with family	an old friend

_____

_____

_____

_____

_____

_____

_____

_____

_____

_____

_____

B. Read your story. Make any changes you wish. You may want to make your story longer. Did you use compound words? Be sure you spelled them correctly.

Unit Two · Rearing Children

READING AND DISCUSSING

A. Talk about it.

Do you have friends who have troubles at home?

B. Read the story.

Running Out

We had troubles at home. My mother ran out on my father. I didn't get on with Dad and his friend Pat. I went to my sister's home in the city.

My sister Jan has a big family, and some of her children got sick. It didn't work out for me to be with them. Jan is a good woman, but she had to send me back home.

I went back—but I didn't go to my father's home. I had no money, no home, and no job. I was looking for trouble, and I got it!

C. Think about it.

Talk about troubles that children like this can get into.

A. Look down and across in the box. Find the words from the first list of words and circle them. Write them.

age
brother
children
find
from
mother
went

s	x	f	d	w	b	w	u
c	h	i	l	d	r	e	n
q	z	n	h	l	o	n	c
y	n	d	p	m	t	t	p
j	u	m	o	t	h	e	r
s	z	v	a	g	e	q	k
z	f	r	o	m	r	l	o

1. ___age___

2. _____

3. _____

4. _____

5. _____

6. _____

7. _____

B. Read the words from the second list of words. Write the words into the puzzle.

father
feel
laugh
lucky
them

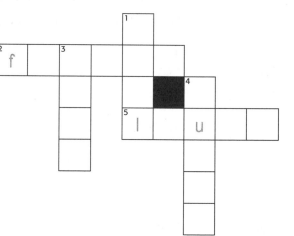

 C. Write a sentence using two or more of the words from the lists.

_____

_____

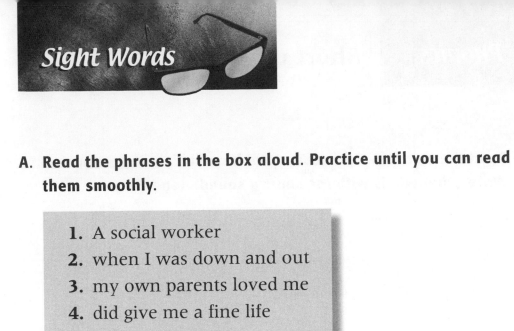

Sight Words

A. Read the phrases in the box aloud. Practice until you can read them smoothly.

> 1. A social worker
> 2. when I was down and out
> 3. my own parents loved me
> 4. did give me a fine life
> 5. who have troubles
> 6. to give me a hug
> 7. When life is bad for me

B. Write the phrases to complete the story.

_____ talked to me about
         1

my troubles. She helped me _____
                       2

_____. She helped me see that _____
                                3

_____. Both my mother and father

_____ at one time.
         4

   My parents are good people _____.
                      5

Sometimes they didn't have time to talk or _____
                                      6

_____. _____
                        7

_____, the social worker helps.

C. Read the story aloud. Practice until you can read it smoothly.

A. Read the words in the list. They all have the short <u>u</u> sound. Write other words with the short <u>u</u> sound. Read them.

up
mug
lug
rug
tug
sun
but
gun
run
us

1. b + us = _____

2. h + ug = _____

3. d + ug = _____

4. n + ut = _____

5. c + up = _____

B. Read the word pairs aloud. Circle the words with the short <u>u</u> sound. Write them.

1. out   up   _____

2. bug   big   _____

3. gut   go   _____

4. buy   bus   _____

5. rat   rut   _____

C. Read the sentences. Circle the words with the short <u>u</u> sound. Write them.

1. Nan had no fun on her own. _____

2. She was nuts to go out on her own. _____

3. Nan was sick, but no one helped her. _____

4. Nan is lucky that she met the social worker.

_____

5. The social worker didn't let Nan cut her family out.

_____

vine
wine
dine
mine
shine
find
my
time
five
fight

A. Read the words in the list. They all have the long i sound.
   Write other words with the long i sound. Read them.

1. n + ine = _____

2. l + ife = _____

3. f + ine = _____

4. l + ight = _____

5. d + ime = _____

B. Read the word pairs aloud. Circle the words with the long i
   sound. Write them.

1. fine   fun   _____

2. pin   pine   _____

3. my   me   _____

4. lake   like   _____

5. lit   light   _____

C. Read the sentences. Circle the words with the long i sound.
   Write them.

1. My mother was feeling sad. _____

2. She got friends to help find me. _____

3. Dad yelled at Jan all the time for sending me home.

   _____

4. Dad was mad that I ran out on him. _____

5. I've got some troubles to work out. _____

A. **Draw a line to match the singular word with its plural form. Write the plural.**

1. life	**a.** women	_____
2. man	**b.** people	_____
3. this	**c.** these	_____
4. woman	**d.** men	_____
5. child	**e.** lives	_____
6. person	**f.** children	_____

B. **Rewrite each sentence so the underlined word or words are singular.**

1. The <u>women</u> looked at me.

_____

2. She helps the <u>children</u> with troubles.

_____

3. <u>These</u> <u>men</u> will help me find a good home.

_____

C. **Read the paragraph. Circle the irregular plurals.**

When I ran out on my dad, I went to the city. Going to the city was a mistake. Some people are no good, and I met a lot of them.

I had no job, no money, and no friends. I went to see a social worker. Social workers help women and men find jobs. They help children find good homes.

I was lucky. The social worker helped me see that life with my dad wasn't that bad. I went back home.

A. Read the rest of the story.

Running Out

I was mad at my parents. I didn't like it when my mother ran out on my dad. I yelled at her to make it work with Dad, but Mom didn't feel that she had a chance.

My mother didn't take me when she went. She had to get a job and set up a home. That is when I went to my sister Jan's home. Jan is a good person, but nine people in one home is a lot. I had to go.

My mistake was in not going to my father's home. Being on my own didn't help me. It didn't help my family. I fell in with a bad group. I got in trouble with the cops.

I'm lucky that I met the social worker. She is helping my parents and me. Can we be a good family? We'll see!

B. Write the answers to the questions. Use complete sentences.

1. Why was Nan mad?

   _____

   _____

2. What problems did Nan have when she went with her sister Jan?

   _____

   _____

   _____

3. Who helped Nan?

   _____

   _____

A. Write your own story. You can use your own idea or find one in the box. You may want to use the phrases below in your story.

Subjects

Home	Trouble	Children
in the city	with parents	all ages
for the holidays	on the job	big hugs
in the country	with friends	lots of love
with the family	work it out	fun to have
to buy	with the cops	sick and well

_____

_____

_____

_____

_____

_____

_____

_____

_____

_____

_____

B. Read your story. Did you tell all that you wanted to tell? Did you write all the plurals correctly? Go back and check.

READING AND DISCUSSING

A. Talk about it.

When you get sick, who helps you out?

B. Read the story.

Finding Help

Our friend Nell Fine is an older woman. She is in good health, but sometimes she has trouble going to the store for food. Nell has no family of her own, so my family helps her out.

Sometime Nell may get sick. At that time, we will get help for her from a nurse or a social worker. Friends and family can do a lot, but in times of trouble one has to get help from these people. It's up to all of us to help Nell.

We have talked to Nell about her health. When she gets sick, these people will help her. She sees that we love her, and that makes her feel good.

C. Think about it.

Have you had a friend with troubles? Could you help? Tell about it.

Review Words

social
worker
glasses
group

A. **Read the words from the first list. Read the phrases. Write the correct word after the phrase that tells about it.**

1. a lot of people _____group_____

2. a helper for people in trouble _____

3. help people see well _____

smoke
smoking
health
chance
about

B. **Look down and across in the box. Find the words from the second list of words and circle them. Write them.**

a	h	q	s	x	z	h
b	d	s	m	o	k	e
o	z	w	o	j	z	a
u	e	x	k	z	q	l
t	w	i	i	u	e	t
c	h	a	n	c	e	h
r	s	b	g	h	i	j

1. _____

2. _____

3. _____

4. _____

5. _____

C. **Use the number code to write the words.**

a	b	c	d	e	f	g	h	i	j	k	l	m
1	2	3	4	5	6	7	8	9	10	11	12	13

n	o	p	q	r	s	t	u	v	w	x	y	z
14	15	16	17	18	19	20	21	22	23	24	25	26

20 1 12 11

_____

6 9 14 5

_____

2 21 20

_____

14 21 18 19 5

_____

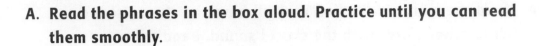

Sight Words

A. Read the phrases in the box aloud. Practice until you can read them smoothly.

> 1. a doctor at the clinic
> 2. about my hip problem
> 3. what the doctor wants
> 4. more hope of getting well
> 5. The doctor said
> 6. when I want to

B. Write the phrases to complete the story.

I go to _____. We talk

_____. I do _____
        2   3

_____. I have _____
                                          4

_____. _____ that
                                  5

someday I will walk _____ without
                              6

feeling bad. The doctor at the clinic has helped me with

my hip problem.

C. Read the story aloud. Practice until you can read it smoothly.

**A. Read the words in the list. They all have the short i sound.
Write other words with the short i sound. Read them.**

hip
zip
tip
clip
ship
big
him
bin
bit
did

1. r + ip = _____

2. d + in = _____

3. s + ip = _____

4. s + ix = _____

5. d + ig = _____

6. w + it = _____

**B. Read the word pairs aloud. Circle the words with the short i
sound. Write them.**

1. fine   fin   _____

2. is   I've   _____

3. fit   find   _____

4. lip   life   _____

5. wine   win   _____

6. kit   kite   _____

**C. Read the sentences. Circle the words with the short i sound.
Write them.**

1. Five people walk to the clinic. _____

2. The people sit for a time. _____

3. Ted has a bit of trouble. _____

4. He has a bad hip. _____

5. The doctor will see Ted. _____

mope
cope
rope
pope
both
home
don't
old
zero
social

A. Read the words in the list. They all have the long o sound. Write other words with the long o sound. Read them.

1. h + ope = _____

2. g + o = _____

3. sm + oke = _____

4. l + ope = _____

5. j + oke = _____

B. Read the word pairs aloud. Circle the words with the long o sound. Write them.

1. pop   pope   _____

2. won't   work   _____

3. do   go   _____

4. on   own   _____

5. cop   cope   _____

C. Read the sentences. Circle the words with the long o sound. Write them.

1. An old woman went to the doctor. _____

2. She had no job. _____

3. The woman had hope for some help. _____

4. The doctor helped her cope with her problems.

_____

5. The nurse will go with the woman to shop. _____

A. Add -er. Write the new words. Read them.

1. work + er = _____

2. buy + er = _____

3. rent + er = _____

4. sell + er = _____

5. talk + er = _____

6. help + er = _____

7. walk + er = _____

8. read + er = _____

9. play + er = _____

10. own + er = _____

B. Finish each sentence with an -er word. Read the sentences.

1. A person who <u>buys</u> is a _____.

2. A person who <u>helps</u> is a _____.

3. A person who <u>owns</u> is an _____.

4. A person who <u>plays</u> is a _____.

C. Write one of the words to complete each sentence. Read the sentences.

helper   walker   worker

1. My hip was bad, so I had to use my _____.

2. The walker was my _____.

3. The nurse is a _____ at the clinic.

Comprehension

A. Read the rest of the story.

Finding Help

Jed Sand was in the clinic today. He was mad at our social worker. She had helped his family find a home. The social worker won't tell Jed where his family is.

Jed isn't good to Kit and his children. Sometimes he hits them. For the time being, Jed's family will have to make a home without him.

I talked to Jed. He has a big problem. He wants to quit being like he is and be good to his family. Sometimes Jed gets mad at work. When he gets home, he takes it out on Kit and the children.

Lots of people have a problem like Jed. We have a group at the clinic to help them. Jed will go into this group. He'll have to cope with his feelings without yelling or hitting people. I hope that someday Jed can be with his family.

B. Write the answers to the questions. Use complete sentences.

1. How did the social worker help Kit and her children?

   _____

   _____

2. What is Jed's problem?

   _____

   _____

3. What can Jed learn in the group?

   _____

   _____

   _____

A. Write your own story. You can use your own idea or find one in the box. You may want to use the phrases below in your story.

Subjects

Health	Friends	Family
in good health	have a good time	helping out
feeling well	going out	in the home
a doctor's work	people I like	what children want
at a clinic	feeling social	more work
eat good food	more to do	what I hope for

_____

_____

_____

_____

_____

_____

_____

_____

_____

_____

B. Read your story. Make any changes in it that you wish. You may want to take out some words and use others. Did you add <u>-er</u> to mean one who does something? Check your spelling of these words.

Handling Social Relationships

READING AND DISCUSSING

A. Talk about it.

What problems do you have with people at work?

B. Read the story.

Team Work

Jen and I like our jobs at Pet Life. We work like a team to find good homes for pets that people cannot care for. The pets are no problem, but a worker named Lee was a big problem at first because he wasn't a team worker. A day went like this:

Jen: Can we go to Home Lane first and get the cat that is in trouble?

Ned: That's a good first stop.

Lee: No, I don't like that plan. We'll go to Sixth and Pine first and get the dogs that need food.

Jen: But Home Lane is . . .

Lee: Your plan is no good, Jen.

Ned: Lee, let's . . .

Lee: Take it from me! My plan is the one that will work.

C. Think about it.

What does Lee do that upsets the people he works with?

A. Read the words in the list. Then write each word under the letter that the word begins with.

hope
trouble
helper
store
hand
takes
see

t	s	h	
_____	_____	_____	_____
_____	_____	_____	

B. Use the number code to write the words.

a	b	c	d	e	f	g	h	i	j	k	l	m
1	2	3	4	5	6	7	8	9	10	11	12	13

n	o	p	q	r	s	t	u	v	w	x	y	z
14	15	16	17	18	19	20	21	22	23	24	25	26

1 12 12

_____

2 15 19 19

_____

7 15 20

_____

14 9 14 5

_____

C. Write the word <u>play</u> for each picture.

1. I went to see
a ____play____.

2. Can you
_____
this?

3. Will you
_____
with me?

Sight Words

A. Read the phrases in the box aloud. Practice until you can read them smoothly.

1. cover the city
2. Day by day
3. load pets
4. need help
5. there is
6. because he does not
7. on the team

B. Write the phrases to complete the story.

Jen, Lee, and I ———————————————— in our
1

work. ————————————, we ————————————
2   3

that ————————————— into our van. The work and
4

the pay are fine, but ————————————— a problem
5

with Lee ———————————————————— work well
6

with people.

He is ——————————————, but he is not a
7

team player.

C. Read the story aloud. Practice until you can read it smoothly.

A. **Read the words in the list. They all have the long <u>a</u> sound. Write other words with the long <u>a</u> sound. Read them.**

day
clay
bake
lake
today
age
mistake
radio
table
they

1. pl + ay = _____

2. m + ake = _____

3. g + ame = _____

4. f + ake = _____

5. t + ape = _____

B. **Read the word pairs aloud. Circle the words with the long <u>a</u> sound. Write them.**

1. mate   mat   _____

2. had   hay   _____

3. said   say   _____

4. eight   end   _____

5. that   they   _____

C. **Read the sentences. Circle the words with the long <u>a</u> sound. Write them.**

1. We will talk to Lee today. _____

2. We have to say what we feel. _____

3. There's no way he will like that! _____

4. Can Lee be a team player? _____

5. Will he wake up to the problems he has on the job?

_____

A. **Read the words in the list. They all have the long <u>e</u> sound.**
   Write other words with the long <u>e</u> sound. Read them.

seed
see
reader
team
heed
eat
we'll
key
he
three

1. w + eed = _____
2. f + eel = _____
3. r + eed = _____
4. d + eed = _____
5. b + eat = _____

B. **Read the word pairs aloud. Circle the words with the long <u>e</u>**
   sound. Write them.

1. nine   need   _____
2. be   bet   _____
3. she   shcll   _____
4. my   me   _____
5. team   ten   _____

C. **Read the sentences. Circle the words with the long <u>e</u> sound.**
   Write them.

1. Lee has problems with work. _____
2. We'll give him some tips. _____
3. Let's work together as a team. _____
4. I hope he will not get mad. _____
5. Let's see if it helps. _____

A. Write the sentences. Add commas where they belong. Then read the sentences.

1. We give our pets homes food and love.

_____

2. We plan talk and drive.

_____

3. The dogs eat jump and run.

_____

4. Lee will you work with us?

_____

5. Jen my way is best.

_____

6. He got his job on June 12 2000.

_____

B. Write sentences of your own. Use commas where they belong.

1. A sentence that separates words in a series

_____

2. A sentence that starts with an introductory word

_____

3. A sentence that gives a date

_____

A. Read the rest of the story.

Team Work

The people on a team make plans as a team. If they don't see eye to eye about the work, they talk about it. They come up with a plan they all feel OK about.

Lee had two big problems. First, he cut in when we talked. Second, he didn't like a plan if it wasn't his plan! This was what we talked to him about. It was no fun to do it. Big problems aren't fun to face. But Jen and I looked Lee in the eye. We talked about the trouble he made for our team. At first, he was mad at us. But in a day or so he was OK.

Talks like this do work. Today we're a team of three. If Lee gives us trouble sometimes, all three of us just laugh!

B. Write the answers to the questions. Use complete sentences.

1. How does a good team work?

_____

_____

2. What did Jen and Ned talk to Lee about?

_____

_____

3. What tips work for a team you're on?

_____

_____

_____

A. Write your own story. You can use your own idea or find one in the box. You may want to use the phrases below in your story.

Subjects

Teamwork	The Way I Feel	Friends
at home	about me	at work
need for it	about my job	helping out
on the job	plans for the day	a need to talk
give all you have	working together	new friends
talk about it	big problems	on the job

_____

_____

_____

_____

_____

_____

_____

_____

_____

_____

B. Read your story. Does it say what you want it to? Check your sentences. Have you used commas in the right places? Make the changes you need.

Unit Five
Volunteering Time

READING AND DISCUSSING

A. Talk about it.

What do you do when you have time on your hands?

B. Read the story.

Time To Give

My job ends at 5 P.M., so I have some time on my hands. I want to feel that I'm using my time to help people. I give three nights to the city's Hot Line.

The Hot Line is a call-in help line. People call with different problems. A parent may call about a child who has run away. A disabled person may need help getting to a clinic, or a father may need food for his family.

I set callers up with our helpers. There are a lot of helpers out there! A Hot Line is about people helping people.

Why do I give time to the Hot Line? I give my time because I called one time when I was in trouble.

C. Think about it.

Do you feel that you use time well?

A. Read the review words. Circle all the vowels.

1. be	**2.** did	**3.** do
4. does	**5.** dog	**6.** eat
7. eyes	**8.** fed	**9.** his
10. mistake	**11.** my	**12.** send

B. Look down and across in the box. Find the words from the list and circle them. Write them.

dog
does
eyes
his
mistake
send

d	o	g	n	i	m	r	l
p	i	l	d	h	i	s	w
v	d	e	s	q	s	v	n
f	o	b	e	x	t	p	e
b	e	k	n	i	a	q	y
l	s	i	d	z	k	w	e
r	j	e	v	c	e	o	s

1. _____
2. _____
3. _____
4. _____
5. _____
6. _____

C. Use the number code to write the words.

a	b	c	d	e	f	g	h	i	j	k	l	m
1	2	3	4	5	6	7	8	9	10	11	12	13

n	o	p	q	r	s	t	u	v	w	x	y	z
14	15	16	17	18	19	20	21	22	23	24	25	26

5 1 20   4 9 4   6 5 4   2 5

_____   _____   _____   _____

Sight Words

A. Read the phrases in the box aloud. Practice until you can read them smoothly.

1. do different things
2. teach women in prison to read
3. has disabled kids come out to the country
4. give time in June
5. they feel it's the right thing to do
6. I learn a lot

B. Write the phrases to complete the story.

People _____ to help
                    1

out. A group of teachers helps _____
                                          2

_____. A baseball team _____
                                                    3

_____

for a day of games, fun, and food. A lot of people

_____ to fix up the
        4

outside of the clinic.

Some people help because _____
                                      5

_____. I feel that by

helping _____.
            6

C. Read the story aloud. Practice until you can read it smoothly.

A. **Read the words in the list. They all have the long i sound. Write other words with the long i sound. Read them.**

right
might
sight
find
time
my
by
like
dime
nine

1. t + ight = _____

2. d + ine = _____

3. f + ive = _____

4. sh + ine = _____

5. l + ight = _____

B. **Read the word pairs aloud. Circle the words with the long i sound. Write them.**

1. I'm   in   _____

2. win   wine   _____

3. fine   fin   _____

4. life   lip   _____

5. dim   dime   _____

C. **Read the sentences. Circle the words with the long i sound. Write them.**

1. Bill likes helping people. _____

2. He works at the Hot Line. _____

3. A lot of calls come in at night. _____

4. Sometimes Bill needs more people to help him.

_____

5. Bill had five calls from one family. _____

June
cute
mule
tube
lose
do
you

A. Read the words in the list. They all have the long u sound as in June or cute. Write other words with the long u sound. Read them.

1. d   +   une   =   _____

2. t   +   une   =   _____

3. pr   +   une   =   _____

4. f   +   ood   =   _____

5. m   +   ood   =   _____

B. Read the word pairs aloud. Circle the words with the long u sound as in June or cute. Write them.

1. use   us   _____

2. mut   mute   _____

3. group   gun   _____

4. who   won't   _____

C. Read the sentences. Circle the words with the long u sound as in June or cute. Write them.

1. Bill and his group fix up run-down homes. _____

2. The homeowners can use Bill's help. _____

3. Owners who have money problems can't pay workers.

_____

4. The owners make food for the workers. _____

5. A group like Bill's can do a lot of good. _____

A. Read the sentences. Circle the verbs that show past time.

Present Time	**Past Time**
1. I do my work.	**1.** I did my work.
2. She is on the job.	**2.** She was on the job.
3. We go out.	**3.** We went out.
4. We take food with us.	**4.** We took food with us.
5. People come for it.	**5.** People came for it.
6. They give it to children.	**6.** They gave it to children.

B. Read the sentences. Circle the verbs. Write <u>present</u> or <u>past</u> in the blank.

1. I give a lot of time to the Hot Line. ___present___

2. I come in at six. _____

3. I go home at ten. _____

4. One time I was there all night. _____

5. Sid came in. _____

6. He gave me a hand with the calls. _____

7. Sid and I are a good team. _____

C. Write three sentences. Use an irregular verb in each sentence.

1. _____

_____

2. _____

_____

3. _____

_____

A. Read the rest of the story.

Time To Give

People who help don't have to be in a group. For some people helping is doing a good deed when they see the need. You might help out when someone's car needs work. Or you might feed a pet when a friend is on a trip.

A lot of people like working with a group. Which group is the one for you?

We all have things we do well. Some of us like working with our hands. Some of us are good at teaching. There are groups for all these needs. One way to find the right group is to call a hot line.

When you lend a helping hand, you will find that a lot of people are doing the same thing. A group of disabled people makes things for a clinic. Then the workers at the clinic see that older people get eyeglasses. The older people then help out with groups of children.

Giving time doesn't pay a dime. But people who give get a lot out of it.

B. Write the answers to the questions. Use complete sentences.

1. What is a hot line?

_____

_____

2. Why do some people give time for no pay?

_____

_____

3. What kinds of groups do you like to work with?

_____

_____

A. Write your own story. You can use your own idea or find one in the box. You may want to use the phrases below in your story.

Subjects

Giving Time	Groups	Hot Lines
have a job	people in the city	talking to people
working at night	my own needs	finding help
time to work	a group I like	people's problems
using time well	family and friends	children in trouble
a good deed	helping out	disabled people

_____

_____

_____

_____

_____

_____

_____

_____

_____

_____

B. Read your story. What can you add? What can you take out? Look for words that show past time. Did you spell them correctly? Draw a line under words you want to look up and check.

READING AND DISCUSSING

A. Talk about it.

How do you feel about people who have on uniforms in the jobs they do?

B. Read the story.

A Job To Do

I have a job as a cop. A lot of people get out of my way when they see my uniform. They don't want to be stopped for running a red light or something like that. To them, a person in a uniform is trouble!

But I see things in a different way. People driving on city roads need to be safe. Sometimes cops like me have to give tickets.

Cops do a lot of things for people on the go. I stop and help people in disabled cars. I help people when they lose their way. I do what I have to do to help people. I see that people who need to, get to a doctor. I'm a friend to people on the go.

C. Think about it.

Talk about the ways that cops can help people.

Review Words

bet
fit
holiday
son

A. Read the words from the first list. Read the phrases. Write the correct word after the phrase that tells about it.

1. a day for fun with family and friends _____

2. take a chance _____

3. feeling healthy _____

4. one of parents' children _____

ad
bigger
hand
no
on
read
upset

B. Read the words from the second list. First write the words that begin with vowels. Then write the words that begin with consonants.

1. _____ _____ _____

2. _____ _____

_____ _____

C. Write the word <u>will</u> for each picture. Use a capital letter to begin a sentence or a name.

1. _____ you   **2.** She is   **3.** _____

dine with me?   reading the   is my friend.

_____.

44

Sight Words

A. Read the phrases in the box aloud. Practice until you can read them smoothly.

> 1. hot days and cold nights
> 2. on the road
> 3. drive well
> 4. mind the rules of the road
> 5. to stop heavy rigs
> 6. trucks carry
> 7. lonely to work

B. Write the phrases to complete the story.

On both _____ 1 _____, a cop

like me is _____ 2 _____. I see that people

_____ 3 _____ and _____ 4 _____

_____. Sometimes I have _____ 5 _____

_____. Some _____ 6 _____ a lot of

heavy goods.

Is it _____ 7 _____ on the road all

the time? No! I love it!

C. Read the story aloud. Practice until you can read it smoothly.

A. Read the words in the list. They all have the short i̲ sound. Write other words with the short i̲ sound. Read them.

dig
lip
into
clinic
sit
bin
sister
sick
fit
zipper

1. f + ig = _____

2. k + in = _____

3. h + ip = _____

4. p + ig = _____

5. b + it = _____

B. Read the word pairs aloud. Circle the words with the short i̲ sound. Write them.

1. din   dine   _____

2. fight   fit   _____

3. will   well   _____

4. gave   give   _____

5. big   bat   _____

C. Read the sentences. Circle the words with the short i̲ sound. Write them.

1. A lot of truckers carry goods to the city.

   _____

2. When I see a disabled truck, I stop to help.

   _____

3. This can take time. _____

4. I helped dig a truck out of the sand. _____

5. I have helped sick people get to a doctor. _____

fold
gold
lonely
pope
social
smoke
old
both
home
zero

A. Read the words in the list. They all have the long o sound. Write other words with the long o sound. Read them.

1. h + old = _____

2. s + old = _____

3. m + ope = _____

4. t + old = _____

5. c + ope = _____

B. Read the word pairs aloud. Circle the words with the long o sound. Write them.

1. hope   hop   _____

2. don't   do   _____

3. no   not   _____

4. bed   bold   _____

5. rip   rope   _____

C. Read the sentences. Circle the words with the long o sound. Write them.

1. Sometimes I go to work at night. _____

2. I use my radio a lot. _____

3. On cold nights I take some hot food with me.

   _____

4. My boss told me that I may have to work on

   some holidays. _____

5. On holidays I want to be home with my family.

   _____

Dropping Final -e
to Add -ed and -ing

A. Drop the final -e. Add -ed. Then add -ing.

1. hope   _____hoped_____   _____hoping_____

2. tape   _____   _____

3. age   _____   _____

4. shine   _____   _____

5. use   _____   _____

6. love   _____   _____

B. Read the sentences. Circle the words that end in -ed and -ing. Write them.

1. I like driving in the city. _____

2. I get my radio tuned in right. _____

3. I used to like smoking in the car, but I gave it up.

_____ _____

4. I'm using my time in different ways. _____

C. Write one of the words to complete each sentence.

loved   taped   hoped   giving   waking

1. I have _____ cars all my life.

2. I _____ to get a job like this.

3. This job is _____ me lots of chances to see the city.

4. I don't like _____ up at 5 A.M.

5. Sometimes I play _____ music in my car.

A. Read the rest of the story.

A Job to Do

I wanted to go on the road because I love driving. But my family needed me at home. They didn't want me to be on the road for days at a time. Being a cop is a good way to do some driving and yet be home some of the time.

I work some nights, some days, and some holidays. But I get lots of time at home. My pay isn't bad, and I have the right to use the clinic when I'm sick.

I've learned a lot about people in my job. Some people are different when they get in a car. They drive like they own the road. They want to fight me when I stop them. I have learned to tune out bad talk. I don't want trouble, but I want people to stay safe.

B. Write the answers to the questions. Use complete sentences.

1. What did this woman want to do for a job?

_____

_____

2. When does the woman work?

_____

_____

3. What are some people like when they get in a car?

_____

_____

_____

A. Write your own story. You can use your own idea or find one in the box. You may want to use the phrases below in your story.

Subjects

Driving	Working at Night	Learning About People
on the road	as a cop	good and bad
in a truck	mopping up	helping out
a fine car	at a clinic	teaching children
heavy rigs	lonely job	loving and learning
driving rules	use the radio	being different

_____

_____

_____

_____

_____

_____

_____

_____

_____

_____

B. Read your story. Did it come out the way you thought it would? Make changes to improve it. Check the words to which you added _-ed_ and _-ing_. Did you drop the _e_ in the right places?

Unit Seven

Working Together for Change

READING AND DISCUSSING

A. Talk about it.

What kind of problems do you have with work and family?

B. Read the story.

A Problem of Time

"Why can't you come to my play?" asked Dale. "You went to see Ted's play."

"Yes, I went to Ted's play," Vee said, "but it was on a weekend. Your play is on a weekday. I can't get out of work."

Dale didn't get it. She wanted her mother to come to the play. She wanted Vee to see how good she was in her role. Ben's parents were coming. Deb's parents would be there. Mad and upset, Dale ran from her mother.

Vee did the dishes on her own. She hated to see Dale's feelings hurt. But she had used all her holidays, and she didn't dare to skip work. She didn't want to lose her job. She had bills to pay. And someone had to be at her spot to do the work if she wasn't there.

C. Think about it.

What is Dale's problem? What is Vee's problem?

A. Circle the vowel in each word if it has a long vowel sound.

1. play   2. about   3. person

4. hope   5. hurt   6. safety

7. see   8. right   9. want

B. Draw a line to match each word and its opposite.

1. hurt   **a.** parents

2. hope   **b.** get rid of

3. children   **c.** here

4. play   **d.** give up

5. want   **e.** work

6. there   **f.** help

C. Write three sentences. Use two or more of the words from the list in each sentence.

1. _____

   _____

   _____

2. _____

   _____

   _____

3. _____

   _____

children
safety
right
want
about
person
hope
hurt
there

Sight Words

A. **Read the phrases in the box aloud. Practice until you can read them smoothly.**

> 1. was beat
> 2. sat together in Jill's garden
> 3. was still
> 4. from the action of the street
> 5. many times
> 6. It will be sad
> 7. have a camera to take photos

B. **Write the phrases to complete the story.**

Vee _____ but she talked to her friend
       1

Jill about Dale's play. They _____
                              2

_____. It _____ there,
                    3

away _____.
            4

Talking with Jill had helped Vee _____.
                                  5

"_____ if you can't go," said Jill.
     6

"We'll have to come up with a plan." Vee nodded.

"Do you _____
                  7

of Dale's play?" asked Jill.

C. **Read the story aloud. Practice until you can read it smoothly.**

53

Unit 7

A. Read the words in the list. They all have the short <u>a</u> sound. Write other words with the short <u>a</u> sound. Read them.

lag
tag
camera
at
bandstand
bad
sat
drag
an
bag

1. n + ag = _____

2. r + an = _____

3. c + at = _____

4. b + and = _____

5. s + ad = _____

B. Read the word pairs aloud. Circle the words with the short <u>a</u> sound. Write them.

1. wag   wig   _____

2. sag   say   _____

3. sand   send   _____

4. meat   mat   _____

5. rag   rig   _____

C. Read the sentences. Circle the words with the short <u>a</u> sound. Write them.

1. I'd like a chance to see the play. _____

2. I have to talk to my boss. _____

3. I can ask him for a different work plan.

_____ _____ _____

4. I will take action on this. _____

5. I will be glad to work it out. _____

wheat	
meat	
beat	
street	
teach	
weed	
we'll	
he	
she	
three	

A. Read the words in the list. They all have the long <u>e</u> sound. Write other words with the long <u>e</u> sound. Read them.

1. s + eat = _____

2. n + eed = _____

3. f + eat = _____

4. r + eed = _____

5. h + eed = _____

6. st + eam = _____

B. Read the word pairs aloud. Circle the words with the long <u>e</u> sound. Write them.

1. neat   net   _____

2. fed   feel   _____

3. ten   treat   _____

4. seed   sell   _____

5. time   team   _____

6. eight   eat   _____

C. Read the sentences. Circle the words with the long <u>e</u> sound. Write them.

1. I want to see Dale's play. _____

2. She has a big role. _____

3. I am needed at work. _____

4. If I got out at three, I could be at the play in time.

_____   _____

A. Read the sentences. Circle the quotation marks. Underline the words that are not spoken.

1. Vee said, "I'm a working parent."

2. "You need some time for Dale," said Jill.

3. "I'll talk to people where I work," said Vee. "I've learned that many of them have the same problem."

B. Write each sentence below. Add quotation marks, commas, and question marks.

1. I like my job said Vee.

   _____

   _____

2. Will your boss give your plan a chance asked Jill.

   _____

   _____

3. I hope so! said Vee.

   _____

   _____

4. My sister has a plan like that at her job she said.

   _____

   _____

5. Vee said I will get together with all the workers and see what we can do.

   _____

   _____

A. Read the rest of the story.

A Problem of Time

Vee learned about different work plans. She liked one plan because it gave workers more time at home. With this job sharing plan, people worked on teams to do a job. The workers all had more time at home, but by sharing the job, they got it done. "This is a good plan for people who have children," said Vee. "They give up some pay for more time with their kids."

Vee talked to the workers in her shop. Many of the women said they would like a job sharing plan. Some of the men wanted it, too. Would their boss go for it?

Vee and Rod went to see Mr. Peat, their boss. There on Mr. Peat's desk was a family photo. It was of his four children in a garden. "You have a big family," said Vee.

"Yes," said her boss. "I would like to spend more time with them."

"Well," said Vee. And she told him about the job sharing plan. "Here's how it works," she said. "I would come in at eight and work to one. Rod would come in at one and work to six. Someone would be on the job all day."

Mr. Peat nodded. "It might be OK," he said. "I'll talk to my boss about it. Maybe I can do it, too!"

B. Write the answers to the questions. Use complete sentences.

1. What was Vee's plan?

   _____

   _____

2. Why did Mr. Peat like the plan?

   _____

   _____

From Reading to Writing

A. Write your own story. You can use your own idea or find one in the box. You may want to use the phrases below in your story.

Subjects

Teams at Work	Taking Photos	Family Needs
a good boss	a good camera	time together
working together	many mistakes	work and play
getting the job done	family times	photos of children
helping out	action shots	music and reading

_____

_____

_____

_____

_____

_____

_____

_____

_____

_____

B. Read your story. Did you use your best ideas? Do you want to add more? In your story, did you use words that people say? Did you use quotation marks, commas, and capital letters in the right way? Check your story.

Answer Key

Unit One

Page 4 **A.** 1. old 2. goods 3. some 4. quit 5. music 6. time **B.** 1. c 2. a 3. b **C.** guitar, plan, trouble, music, quit, lose

Page 5 **B.** 1. see the value of Nell's tapes 2. take his time 3. records on tape what is going on 4. has a cold 5. in a shop that sells videos

Page 6 **A.** 1. bend 2. let 3. tent 4. red 5. shell **B.** 1. fell 2. sell 3. bet 4. fed 5. web **C.** 1. Ted, get 2. end 3. tell, Ted 4. well 5. help, Ted, when

Page 7 **A.** 1. cake 2. page 3. fake 4. shape 5. stage **B.** 1. sake 2. tables 3. wage 4. cape 5. play **C.** 1. makes 2. tapes 3. takes 4. tapes 5. plays, tapes

Page 8 **A.** 1. sunset 2. catwalk 3. sandlot 4. homesick 5. bedtime 6. outlet 7. workout **B.** 1. some, times 2. sun, down 3. up, set 4. in, side 5. video, tape 6. some, where 7. to, night **C.** 1. videotape, upset, tonight, upset, sometimes, workout, inside

Page 9 **B.** 1. Mrs. Lake likes to read, but she doesn't see well. 2. Ted helps Mrs. Lake. 3. Ted buys books on tape for Mrs. Lake.

Unit Two

Page 12 **A.** Order may vary. 1. age 2. brother 3. children 4. find 5. from 6. mother 7. went **B.** 1. feel 2. father 3. them 4. lucky 5. laugh

Page 13 **B.** 1. A social worker 2. when I was down and out 3. my own parents loved me 4. did give me a fine life 5. who have troubles 6. to give me a hug 7. When life is bad for me

Page 14 **A.** 1. bus 2. hug 3. dug 4. nut 5. cup **B.** 1. up 2. bug 3. gut 4. bus 5. rut **C.** 1. fun 2. nuts 3. but 4. lucky 5. cut

Page 15 **A.** 1. nine 2. life 3. fine 4. light 5. dime **B.** 1. fine 2. pine 3. my 4. like 5. light **C.** 1. My 2. find 3. time 4. I 5. I've

Page 16 **A.** 1. e, lives 2. d, men 3. c, these 4. a, women 5. f, children 6. b, people **B.** 1. The woman looked at me. 2. She helps the child with troubles. 3. This man will help me find a good home. **C.** people, women, men, children

Page 17 **B.** 1. Nan was mad because her parents were breaking up. 2. Jan's family was too big. 3. The social worker helped Nan.

Unit Three

Page 20 **A.** 1. group 2. social worker 3. glasses **B.** Order may vary. 1. smoke 2. health 3. about 4. chance 5. smoking **C.** talk, but, fine, nurse

Page 21 **B.** 1. a doctor at the clinic 2. about my hip problem 3. what the doctor wants 4. more hope of getting well 5. The doctor said 6. when I want to

Page 22 **A.** 1. rip 2. din 3. sip 4. six 5. dig 6. wit **B.** 1. fin 2. is 3. fit 4. lip 5. win 6. kit **C.** 1. clinic 2. sit 3. bit 4. hip 5. will

Page 23 **A.** 1. hope 2. go 3. smoke 4. lope 5. joke **B.** 1. pope 2. won't 3. go 4. own 5. cope **C.** 1. old 2. no 3. hope 4. cope 5. go

Page 24 **A.** 1. worker 2. buyer 3. renter 4. seller 5. talker 6. helper 7. walker 8. reader 9. player 10. owner **B.** 1. buyer 2. helper 3. owner 4. player **C.** 1. walker 2. helper 3. worker

Page 25 **B.** 1. The social worker helped Kit and the children by finding them a home. 2. Jed gets mad and hits his family and yells at them. 3. Jed can learn to cope with being mad. He can learn to quit hitting people and yelling.

Unit Four

Page 28 **A.** h: hope, helper, hand; s: store, see; t: trouble, takes **B.** all, boss, got, nine **C.** 1. play 2. play 3. play

Page 29 **B.** 1. cover the city 2. Day by day 3. load pets 4. need help 5. there is 6. because he does not 7. on the team

Page 30 **A.** 1. play 2. make 3. game 4. fake 5. tape **B.** 1. mate 2. hay 3. say 4. eight 5. they **C.** 1. today 2. say 3. way 4. player 5. wake

Page 31 **A.** 1. weed 2. feel 3. reed 4. deed 5. beat **B.** 1. need 2. be 3. she 4. me 5. team **C.** 1. Lee 2. We'll 3. team 4. he 5. see

Page 32   A. 1. We give our pets homes, food, and love. 2. We plan, talk, and drive. 3. The dogs eat, jump, and run. 4. Lee, will you work with us? 5. Jen, my way is best. 6. He got his job on June 12, 2000.

Page 33   B. 1. A good team talks and plans together. 2. They talked about the way he cut in and how he liked just his own plans. 3. Answers will vary.

Unit Five

Page 36   A. 1. b(e) 2. d(i)d 3. d(o) 4. d(o)(e)s 5. d(o)g 6. (e)(a)t 7. (e)y(e)s 8. f(e)d 9. h(i)s 10. m(i)st(a)k(e) 11. m(y) 12. s(e)nd **B.** Order may vary. 1. dog 2. his 3. does 4. send 5. mistake 6. eyes **C.** eat, did, fed, be

Page 37 1. do different things 2. teach women in prison to read 3. has disabled kids come out to the country 4. give time in June 5. they feel it's the right thing to do 6. I learn a lot

Page 38   A. 1. tight 2. dine 3. five 4. shine 5. light **B.** 1. I'm 2. wine 3. fine 4. life 5. dime **C.** 1. likes 2. Line 3. night 4. Sometimes 5. five

Page 39   A. 1. dune 2. tune 3. prune 4. food 5. mood **B.** 1. use 2. mute 3. group 4. who **C.** 1. group 2. use 3. who 4. food 5. group, do

Page 40   A. 1. did 2. was 3. went 4. took 5. came 6. gave **B.** 1. give, present 2. come, present 3. go, present 4. was, past 5. came, past 6. gave, past 7. are, present

Page 41   B. 1. A hot line is a telephone call-in service that helps people with troubles solve their problems. 2. People give time for no pay because they feel good when they help people. 3. Answers will vary.

Unit Six

Page 44   A. 1. holiday 2. bet 3. fit 4. son **B.** 1. ad, on, upset 2. bigger, hand, no, read **C.** 1. Will 2. will 3. Will

Page 45   B. 1. hot days and cold nights 2. on the road 3. drive well 4. mind the rules of the road 5. to stop heavy rigs 6. trucks carry 7. lonely to work

Page 46   A. 1. fig 2. kin 3. hip 4. pig 5. bit **B.** 1. din 2. fit 3. will 4. give 5. big **C.** 1. city 2. disabled 3. This 4. dig 5. sick

Page 47   A. 1. hold 2. sold 3. mope 4. told 5. cope **B.** 1. hope 2. don't 3. no 4. bold 5. rope **C.** 1. go 2. radio 3. cold 4. told 5. home

Page 48   A. 1. hoped, hoping 2. taped, taping 3. aged, aging 4. shined, shining 5. used, using 6. loved, loving **B.** 1. driving 2. tuned 3. used, smoking 4. using **C.** 1. loved 2. hoped 3. giving 4. waking 5. taped

Page 49   B. 1. The woman wanted to drive for a job. 2. She works some nights, some days, and some holidays. 3. Some people drive like they own the road.

Unit Seven

Page 52   A. 1. pl(a)y 4. h(o)pe 6. s(a)fet(y) 7. s(e)e 8. r(i)ght **B.** 1. f, help 2. d, give up 3. a, parents 4. e, work 5. b, get rid of 6. c, here

Page 53   B. 1. was beat 2. sat together in Jill's garden 3. was still 4. from the action of the street 5. many times 6. It will be sad 7. have a camera to take photos

Page 54   A. 1. nag 2. ran 3. cat 4. band 5. sad **B.** 1. wag 2. sag 3. sand 4. mat 5. rag **C.** 1. chance 2. have 3. can, ask, plan 4. action 5. glad

Page 55   A. 1. seat 2. need 3. feat 4. reed 5. heed 6. steam **B.** 1. neat 2. feel 3. treat 4. seed 5. team 6. eat **C.** 1. see 2. She 3. needed 4. three, be

Page 56   A. 1. <u>Vee</u> <u>said</u>, ⁞I'm a working parent.⁞ 2. ⁞You <u>need</u> some time for Dale,⁞ <u>said</u> <u>Jill</u>. 3. ⁞I'll talk to people where I work,⁞ <u>said</u> <u>Vee</u>. ⁞I've learned that many of them have the same problem. ⁞ **B.** 1. "I like my job," said Vee. 2. "Will your boss give your plan a chance?" asked Jill. 3. "I hope so!" said Vee. 4. "My sister has a plan like that at her job," she said. 5. Vee said, "I will get together with all the workers and see what we can do."

Page 57   B. 1. She wanted to introduce job sharing at her shop. 2. He also wanted more time to spend with his family.

60